new

Hennie Zellenrath

FORTE PUBLISHERS

Contents

Fifth printing May 2004
ISBN 90 5877 212 8

This is a publication from
Forte Publishers BV
P.O. Box 1394
3500 BJ Utrecht
The Netherlands

For more information about the creative books available from Forte Uitgevers:
www.hobby-party.com

Publisher: Marianne Perlot
Editor: Hanny Vlaar
Photography and digital image editing: Fotografie Gerhard Witteveen, Apeldoorn, the Netherlands
Cover and inner design:
Studio Herman Bade BV, Baarn, the Netherlands

Preface

The Coluzzle template is an excellent cutting aid to make cards.
I use a template for whatever card technique I use. After the success of
the technique of making an incision, folding and finishing the card with
paper of a contrasting colour or some nice pictures, there is now a
completely new book for the use of the Coluzzle template.

These ten chapters will show you that you can do almost anything
with a Coluzzle template to make greetings cards. For very little
money, you will be able to make many different cards from old and
new pictures, good quality paper and, of course, the basic materials
required to make cards. See the chapter Cards from scraps to see
what you can do with scrap pieces of card.

I hope this book gives your fantasies a creative impulse. You can do
almost anything using the basic techniques. So let the ideas flow! I
hope you enjoy making the cards as much as I enjoyed designing
them.

Hennie Zellenrath

Hennie ☺

Techniques

Carefully read the instructions and the tips on page 7 and look at the Step-by-step photographs before starting.

1. The templates, a knife and a mat.

The correct materials are essential if you wish to be successful with Coluzzle. Remove the protective layer from both sides of the template. Stick down the four sides of the template using masking tape and place the knife vertically in one of the grooves. Push the knife through the groove, but do not add any more pressure. Cut away from yourself. If you cut towards yourself, you have the tendency to steer the knife, and that is not the intention. The connecting pieces on the template are the barriers and the openings are the grooves. The grooves are counted from the outside to the inside. Groove 1 is, therefore, the outer groove. Always place a piece of photocopy paper between the card and the mat (see photograph 1). Cut through the barriers using an Art knife or a pair of scissors. If using scissors, cut the barriers in a clockwise direction from underneath the pattern.

2. Making window cards and frames.

To determine the size of the opening, place the transparent template on the picture or photograph that you wish to use. Do not use groove 1, because this is used for the frame. If groove 2 is the correct size for the opening, then cut along that groove. Next, cut grooves 1 and 2 in card of a contrasting colour and stick the frame around the opening using photo glue.

3. Leaving the barriers in place.

Instead of making windows, you can also cut the strips out. When doing so, make sure you never use the groove on the outside.
For example, cut grooves 2 and 3 from barrier to barrier. Remove the template and use a ruler and a knife (not the Coluzzle knife) to cut through the barriers. The strip will fall out and you will be left with an opening. You can do this a number of times on the card, so long as there is a whole strip between each one. Another possibility is to cut out a large section along the barriers. You can see this effect very well with the window cards. To do so, cut along one groove, remove the template, place a ruler along the barriers and cut an opening on both sides. It is even nicer if you also draw vertical barriers on the template using a felt-tip pen to make four open sections (see photograph 2).

1. Coluzzle template, Coluzzle knife, masking tape and photocopy paper.

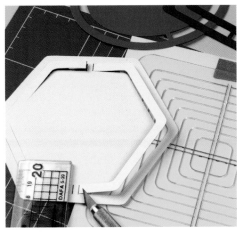

2. Cut from barrier to barrier and leave the barrier in place.

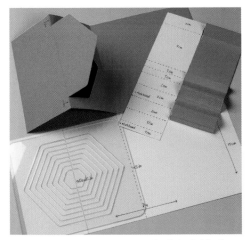

3. Making a standing card which is folded forwards and the stand.

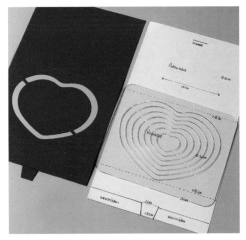

4. Making a peephole card.

4. Cutting a line of patterns following the last technique described in point 3.

I have done this in Tying ribbons. Place the first template to be cut out on the card with the barriers exactly in the middle of the card (draw a pencil line to determine the middle). Cut along the indicated groove. Move the template so that there is a groove between the two patterns. If you do not do this, the openings will join up and that is not what you want. In this way, you will make an open border through which you can, for example, thread a ribbon.

5. A nice technique is to make standing cards which are folded forwards.

A shape cut out from a Coluzzle template sticks out above the folded section. Finish this card with a number of different decorations and scraps from the template used. Since this card will not stand up by itself, you will have to make a stand (see photograph 3).

6. Peephole cards

Photograph 4 shows the method to make a peephole card. These cards are easy to make and they have a real peephole effect. For these cards, the grooves are cut out and the barriers are left in place.

7. Save all the scraps in a box.

Never throw anything away! You can use various borders, frames and other scraps to produce a unique card. Every card will then be different. Adjust the size of the card so that the largest shape you have fits into the card and find some matching colours to use. Stick a picture on the card using photo glue to finish it off and your card will be admired by everybody.

8. There are also intermediate templates for the oval and circle shapes.

These templates are called Companions. You can combine both of these templates (by first using one template and then the other) to make narrow grooves or to make one groove on one side of the card and another groove on the other side. This technique is used for the hatch cards.

Materials

- Card: 220 gram A4 sheets (Artoz)
- Large square cards (16.5 x 16.5) (Artoz)
- Coluzzle templates: circle, circle Companion, oval, oval Companion, narrow oval, hexagon, diamond, heart, star, square and rectangle
- Coluzzle mat and Coluzzle pivoting knife
- Various cutting sheets
- Mirrored card in various colours
- Art knife and cutting mat
- Ruler with a metal cutting edge (Securit)
- Silhouette scissors

- Embossing pen
- Gel pen in various colours
- Circle distance punch or Prym punch
- Gold and silver line stickers
- Satin ribbon (3 mm) in various colours
- Transparent ribbon in various colours
- Masking tape
- Folding tool
- Black thread
- 3D glue/foam tape, nozzle
- Double-sided adhesive tape (9 mm and 12 mm)
- Sparkles glitter writer
- Photo glue, pencil and rubber

Tips

1. Stick all four sides of the template to the card using masking tape.
2. Place (photocopy) paper between the card and the mat to prevent the back of the card from fraying.
3. An easy way to cut away the barriers is to cut them through from the back of the card using silhouette scissors (in a clockwise direction).
4. Use a scrap piece of card which is similar to the card you wish to use to make the card to see which side gives the nicest incision, because the front and back of the card can give a different result.
5. Stand or sit directly above the card, hold the knife upright and push the knife away from you along the groove from barrier to barrier. Rotate everything and repeat the procedure.
6. If the cut is frayed, remove the fray using fine sandpaper.
7. Sometimes, the knife may cut a rough edge in the template. If so, remove it with sandpaper.
8. Use the outer edge of the template as a cutting edge. Use the Art knife, which is excellent for all types of card making.
9. If, for some reason or other, the barriers do not join up, make the cuts slightly longer. Nobody will notice.

Viewing holes

You will not be able to stop looking at these cards.

General information

Take two A4 sheets of card. Use the total length as the width (approximately 29.7 cm) and cut 1 cm from the width of one sheet. Score the other sheet 1 cm from the side and stick double-sided adhesive tape on it. Stick both cards together and score the middle of both cards (at approximately 14.3 cm). Fold this into a zigzag shape and cut the card to a height of 14.3 cm. You have now made a square card which consists of four separate parts.

Cut groove 2 in the front of the card, cut groove 3 in the second section and cut groove 4 in the third section. Cut frames out of a card of a contrasting colour using grooves 1 and 2 and grooves 3 and 4. Use photo glue to stick the largest frame on the front of the card and the smallest frame on the third section. The second section does not get a frame. Cut groove 3 in the background sheet and stick this on the rear card. Stick pictures in front of the three openings using photo glue. Use 3D glue to stick the pictures on the front section. Regularly hold the card at eye level to look at the depth effect.

1. Working in the garden

A4 card: 2x mango (575) and 1x crimson (549) • Cutting sheets: 3D 389 and 3D 392 • Background sheet: 3DA 3307 • Brown gel pen • Oval Coluzzle template

The card is mango and the frames are red. The table and the flowers in the background are raised using 3D glue.

2. Lazing in the garden

A4 card: 2x honey yellow (243) and 1x dark green (309) • Cutting sheet: 3D 388 • Background sheet: 3DA 3305 • Gold gel pen • Circle Coluzzle template

The card is yellow and the frames are green.

3. Down on the farm

A4 card: 2x birch green (305) and 1x pine green (339) • Cutting sheets: 3D 390 and 3D 391 • Background sheet: 3DA 3306 • Hexagon Coluzzle template

The card is light green and the frames are dark green.

4. Sun, sea and sand

A4 card: 2x royal blue (427) and 1x white (211) • Cutting sheets: 3D 394 and 3D 395 • Background sheet: 3DA 3308 • White gel pen • Square Coluzzle template

The card is blue and the frames are white.

1.

2.

3.

4.

Cards with bows

Tie the cards into triangular prisms, open them up and read the personal message.

General information

Cut a card (29.7 x 13.5 cm) and score a line 9.1 cm from both sides. The middle section will then be approximately 11.5 cm wide. Place the Coluzzle template with the barriers vertically on the scored lines and cut groove 1 only in the side flaps. Do not cut anything out. Cut the frame out of the other coloured card by cutting along grooves 1 and 2. Cut this in half so that you have a frame for both side flaps. Stick them on the card using photo glue. Stick some design paper, a frame and a picture on the middle section. The front section is made from a couple of template shapes stuck together, which are tied to the card with two bows. Use the Prym punch to make holes on both sides of the front section. Place the front section on the side flap sections which have been cut out and folded forwards. Push a pencil through the punched out holes to indicate where the holes on the side flaps must be located. Use ribbons to tie the different sections together. Fold the remaining part of the side flaps backwards. Punch holes 1.5 cm from the corners and tie them together to make a triangular prism. Untie the rear ribbon if you wish to post this card.

1. Wedding card

A4 card: fawn (241) and gold mirrored card • Cutting sheet: 3D 357 • More than Memories background sheet: marriage • Coluzzle templates: heart and oval Companion • Light yellow satin ribbon • Gold line sticker

This card is fawn. The frames are made from mirrored card. Use groove 2 of the heart template on the side flaps and use grooves 2 and 3 for the frame. For the middle section, cut grooves 1 and 2 of the oval Companion in the gold card. For the front section, cut groove 3 in the gold card, groove 4 in the fawn card and groove 5 in the gold card. Decorate the gold borders with line stickers.

2. Pink birth card

A4 card: pink (481) and wine red (519) • Baby cutting sheets: AK 019 and AK 021 • Oval Coluzzle template • Pink satin ribbon

The card is pink and the frames are wine red. See the instructions given for the blue birth card, but use groove 2 for the side flaps and place the template sideways. Cut the frame using grooves 2 and 3. Cut grooves 1 and 2 for the middle section. For the front section, cut groove 3 in the red card, groove 4 in the pink card and groove 5 in the red card.

3. Blue birth card

A4 card: royal blue (427) and pastel blue (413) • Baby cutting sheets: AK 019 and AK 021 • Circle Coluzzle template and circle Companion • Light blue satin ribbon • Prym punch

For the side flaps, cut groove 1 of the circle Companion in pastel blue card. For the frame, cut grooves 1 and 2 in royal blue card. For the middle section, cut grooves 1 and 2 of the normal circle template in blue card. For the front section, use the normal circle template and cut

groove 2 in blue card, groove 4 in pastel blue card and groove 5 in blue card. Stick everything on the card using photo glue.

4. Congratulations

A4 card: crimson (549) and honey yellow (243) • Shake-It cutting sheet: IT 331 • More than Memories background sheet: holiday • Rectangle Coluzzle template • Brick red satin ribbon

The card is honey yellow and the frames are crimson. For the side flaps, cut groove 3 of the template sideways. Cut the frame using grooves 3 and 4. For the middle section, cut grooves 3 and 4 of the template lengthways. For the front section, cut groove 5 in red paper, groove 6 in yellow paper and groove 7 in red paper.

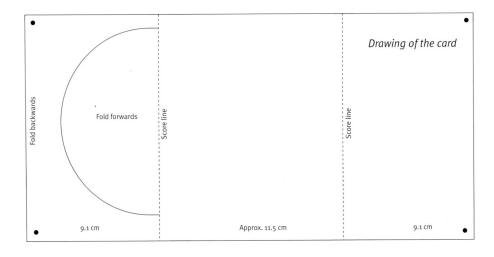

Drawing of the card

Fold backwards

Fold forwards

Score line

Score line

9.1 cm

Approx. 11.5 cm

9.1 cm

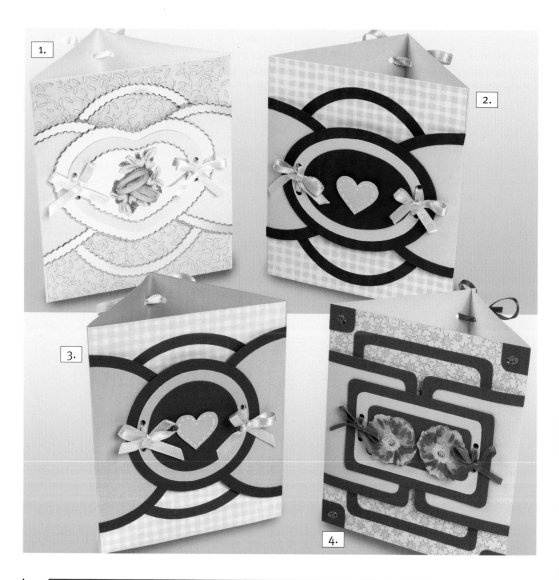

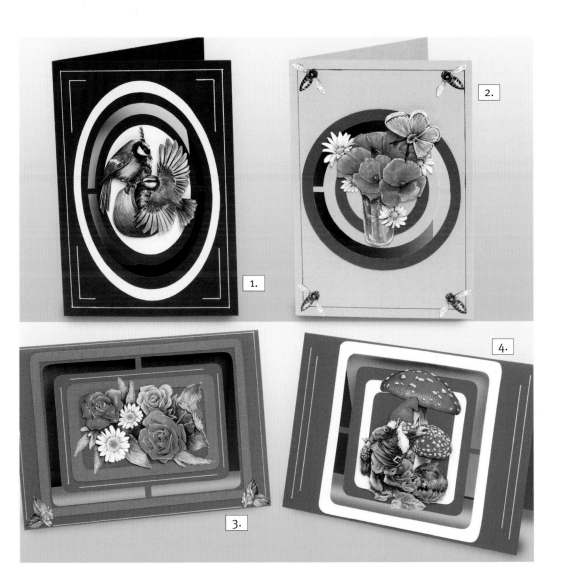

Four seasons

A suitable card for

each season

General information

The double cards measure 14.8 x 10.5 cm. The card of the contrasting colour that remains after the grooves have been cut is stuck in the card (see Techniques, point 3). Make the pictures 3D according to the cutting instructions (pages 22, 23 and 27) and draw decorative lines using a gel pen.

1. Christmas

A4 card: dark blue (417) and white (211) • Narrow oval Coluzzle template • Picturel cutting sheet: 505 • White gel pen

Cut grooves 2 and 3 in blue card and cut the strips out along the barriers. Cut grooves 1 and 2 in white card to make a frame. Cut groove 5 in white card and stick this on the middle section.

2. Spring

A4 card: royal blue (427) and pastel blue (413) • Circle Companion • Picturel cutting sheet: 514 • Blue gel pen

Cut grooves 3 and 4 in pastel blue card and cut the strips out along the barriers. Cut the frame in royal blue card using grooves 2 and 3. Stick it on the card using photo glue. Cut grooves 5 and 6 in the same blue card and stick this in the middle section. Do not forget to use the stamens as antennae for the butterfly.

3. Summer

A4 card: crimson (549) and pine green (339) • Rectangle Coluzzle template • Picturel cutting sheet: 506 • Gold gel pen

Cut grooves 3 and 4 in a horizontal red card and cut the strips out along the barriers. Cut grooves 5 and 6 and grooves 2 and 3 in green card (make the inside of the second frame slightly smaller) and stick them on the card.

4. Autumn

A4 card: red (517) and white (211) • Square Coluzzle template • Picturel cutting sheet: 514 • White gel pen

Cut grooves 3 and 4 in a horizontal red card and cut the strips out along the barriers. Cut grooves 2 and 3 and grooves 5 and 6 in white card and stick them on the card.

Peephole cards

A peephole card can be made for every occasion.

General information

Follow the instructions given in Techniques, point 6 and look at Step-by-step photograph 4 (see page 23). Stick mirrored card against the back in the card and stick the 3D background decorations on this.

1. Beach peephole card

A4 card: royal blue (427) and blue mirrored card • Heart Coluzzle template • White gel pen • Marij Rahder beach panorama: 2256

Place the template on the front of the card approximately 1.5 cm from the bottom score line and cut grooves 2 and 3. Cut the strips out along the barriers. Cut all the way around groove 4.

2. Christmas forest peephole card

A4 card: dark green (309) and silver mirrored card • Diamond Coluzzle template • Marij Rahder deer panorama • Silver line stickers • Silver gel pen • Sparkles glitter writer

Place half of the diamond template lengthways on the front of the card. Cut grooves 2 and 3, leaving the barriers in place. Cut all of groove 4 in the middle section. Remain 1.5 cm from the bottom score line and use a ruler to cut out the shape. Add some glitter writer to the snow.

3. Garden peephole card

A4 card: birch green (305) and green mirrored card • Rectangle Coluzzle template • Marij Rahder magical garden panorama: 2254

Place the template on the front of the card with the barriers in a vertical position. Cut grooves 2 and 3, leaving the barriers in place. Cut up to 1.5 cm above the score line at the bottom. Cut groove 4 until 1.5 cm above the bottom score line. Use a knife and a ruler to cut the card out along this line. The entire template will not fit on the card. Stick green mirrored card (15 x 9.3 cm) in the card until above the incision.

4. Ice fun peephole card

A4 card: white (211) and silver mirrored card • Oval Coluzzle template • Marij Rahder ice fun panorama: 2290 • Silver gel pen • Sparkles glitter writer

Place the oval template sideways on the front of the card. Cut grooves 1 and 2, leaving the barriers in place, and cut groove 3 as an opening until 1.5 cm from the score line. Decorate the picture with the glitter writer.

1.

2.

3.

4.

Standing cards

Use a stand so that these

cards remain upright.

General information

Follow the instructions given in Techniques, point 5 and look at Step-by-step photograph 3. Once the card has been cut to the correct size, you will be left with a 6 cm wide strip, which you can use to make the stand (see page 30). Decorate the card with frames of different colours and different sizes.

Make the pictures 3D according to the cutting instructions.

1. Christmas gnome

A4 card: pine green (339) and wine red (519)
• Rectangle Coluzzle template • Cutting sheet: 3D 369 • Silver line stickers • Sparkles glitter writer • Background sheet: 3DA 3302
Cut half a rectangle from green card using groove 2. Cut out the entire shape in red card using groove 2. Cut a wide frame out of green paper using grooves 3 and 5 and stick it on the red rectangle. Stick the winter forest on the background together with a red frame made from grooves 2 and 3 and a green frame made from

grooves 5 and 6. Decorate the card with the glitter writer, the line stickers and stick scraps from the rectangular shapes in the bottom corners.

2. Lambs

A4 card: royal blue (427) and birch green (375)
• Cloud paper • Hexagon Coluzzle template • Cutting sheet: 3D 375
Use the hexagon template as described for the sunflower card. Cut half of groove 1 in blue card and cut all of groove 1 in green card. Cut a wide frame in the blue card using grooves 2 and 4 and stick this on the card at an angle. Stick cloud paper (14 x 14 cm) on the background and

stick a green frame on this which has been made using grooves 2 and 3 and a blue frame which has been made using grooves 5 and 6. Use grooves 6 and 7 for the bottom corners.

3. Sunflower card

A4 card: sunny yellow (247) and black (219) • Bee paper • Oval Coluzzle template • Cutting sheet: 3D 342

Place the middle of the oval template sideways on the pencil line and cut the top half of groove 1 (if there are any barriers, cut them through). Score the sides and fold the front half forwards; the half cut out template will now stick upwards. Note: the pencil line going over the template shape will not be scored, only the other pencil lines on the side. Rub out the pencil line. Cut all of groove 1 in black card and stick it on the yellow background. Cut grooves 2

and 4 in yellow card to make a wide frame and stick this on the black oval. Stick bee paper (14 x 14 cm) on the background. Cut grooves 2 and 3 in black card and grooves 5 and 6 in yellow card to make frames and stick these on the card lengthways. Cut grooves 6 and 7 in black card

and cut the frame in pieces for the bottom corners. Stick the first narrow strip of the stand behind the front section, stick the second strip with adhesive tape behind the second section and the long strip at the back of the card.

4. Cat in a basket

A4 card: white (211) and red (517) • Cat cutting sheet • Heart Coluzzle template • Cutting sheet: 3D FK 1202 • White gel pen • Black glitter pen

Cut half of the heart shape in red card using groove 1. Cut all of the heart shape in white card using groove 1. Make a wide red frame using grooves 2 and 4. Make a black heart using groove 5 and stick everything on the card. Use the black glitter pen to draw along the outer edge of the largest white heart, otherwise the colour will be lost against the background. Stick the cat cutting sheet (14 x 14 cm) on the background and stick a red heart made using grooves 2 and 3 and a black heart made using grooves 4 and 5 on this. Cut out two black hearts using groove 7 and stick these in the bottom corners. Decorate the card using the white gel pen.

Tying ribbons

Tie an attractive ribbon

through the open border.

General information
This technique is described in Techniques, point 4. Make a double card which measures 23 x 16.5 cm. Place the card horizontally and draw a vertical pencil line through the middle. The barriers will be positioned on this line. Draw a horizontal pencil line 3.2 cm from the bottom. The middle of the first shape to be cut out is where the horizontal and vertical lines cross. Next, place the template on the left and right-hand sides and cut the template two more times. The strips are made from card of a contrasting colour. First, thread the ribbon through the card and then stick a strip of paper behind it. Complete shapes of the template are stuck on the top strip and they are decorated with pictures. The bottom strip is accentuated using line stickers. Punch a hole in the middle at the top of the front of the card and punch holes 1 cm on either side of this. Thread a ribbon through the holes and tie it into a bow.

1. Autumn card
A4 card: crimson (549) and fawn (241) • Hexagon Coluzzle template • Cognac transparent ribbon • Gold line stickers • Shake-It cutting sheet: IT 322
Cut the hexagon three times out of fawn card using groove 7. Thread the ribbon through it and stick a red strip (16.5 x 5.5 cm) underneath. The red strip at the top of the card measures 15.5 x 5.5 cm.

2. Blue birth card
A4 card: royal blue (427) and pastel blue (413) • Square Coluzzle template • Blue transparent ribbon
Cut out three squares according to the instructions using groove 7. There is no room on the sides to cut half of the template. Therefore, cut two extra 2 mm wide grooves so that the ribbon can be hidden neatly behind the card. Stick a blue strip (16.5 x 6 cm) underneath. Stick a strip (15.5 x 5.5 cm) at the top. Stick three squares on this strip which have been cut out of light blue card using groove 7. Stick pictures on the squares. Stick a strip (15.5 x 1 cm) on the bottom of the card.

3. Pink birth card
A4 card: pink (481) and wine red (519) • Circle Companion • Baby cutting sheets: AK 019 and AK 020 • Silver line stickers • Pink transparent ribbon • Circle distance punch • Double-sided adhesive tape
Place the circle template as indicated in the instructions on the card and cut groove 7.

1.

2.

3.

4.

Cut the shapes out along the barriers. Move the template to the right so that groove 6 joins up with the cut out opening and cut groove 7 again. Repeat this on the left-hand side.

Cut half a shape plus an extra 2 mm after the barrier out of the remaining space on the left and right-hand sides. Thread the ribbon through the card and secure it to the back of the card using double-sided adhesive tape. Stick a strip of red card (16.5 x 5 cm) underneath. Stick a strip of red card (15.5 x 6 cm) at the top of the card. Cut out three pink circles using groove 6 and stick pictures on them. Finish the bottom of the card with a strip of card (1.3 x 15.5 cm) which is decorated with silver line stickers.

Drawing for the hatch cards

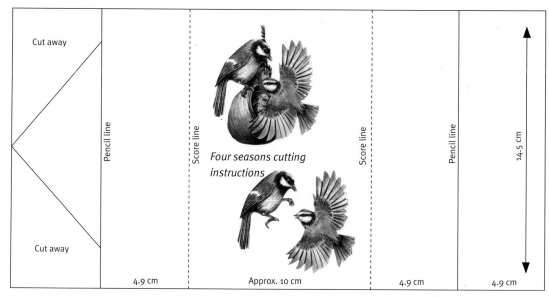

Cut away

Cut away

Pencil line

Score line

Four seasons cutting instructions

Score line

Pencil line

14.5 cm

4.9 cm

Approx. 10 cm

4.9 cm

4.9 cm

4. Spring card

A4 card: sunny yellow (247) and yellow (275)
• Narrow oval Coluzzle template • Yellow transparent ribbon • Gold line stickers • Shake-It cutting sheet: IT 347

Cut groove 7 in yellow card so that three ovals fit next to each other. Thread the ribbon through and stick it to the back of the card. Stick a light yellow card (16.5 x 5 cm) underneath. Stick a light yellow strip (15.5 x 6 cm) at the top of the card and stick on the three ovals which were cut out using groove 7. Stick a light yellow strip (15.5 x 1.3 cm) at the bottom of the card.

Drawing for the viewing hole cards

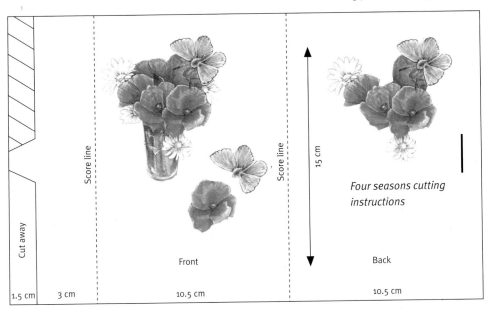

Four seasons cutting instructions

Cut away · Score line · Front · Score line · 15 cm · Back

1.5 cm · 3 cm · 10.5 cm · 10.5 cm

Scenes

Make an attractive scene inside

and on the card.

General information

Cut two differently coloured cards (25.5 x 16.5 cm) and score them in the middle. Score the front card 4 cm from the left and right-hand sides. Place the middle of the Coluzzle template on the middle score line of the front card and cut groove 2. Make the frame from the same colour card as the rear card using grooves 1 and 2. Stick the frame around the opening and score the frame where it lies on the score line.

If you wish, stick these pieces down using double-sided adhesive tape. Stick the cards together. Stick pictures on the card, making some of them 3D. Stick a black thread against the inner card using adhesive tape and attach a Coluzzle shape with a picture on both sides.

1. Mice houses

A4 card: crimson (549) and fawn (241) • Square Coluzzle template • Red glitter pen • Cutting sheets: AK 001 and 002

Make the card according to the instructions and hang the washing on the thread.

2. Christmas card

A4 card: dark blue (417), pastel blue (413) and silver mirrored card • Star Coluzzle template • Cutting sheets: AK 005 and AK 006 • Mini cutting sheet: 3D AM 1003 • White gel pen • Black thread

Make the card according to the instructions. Cut out two small stars and stick them together with the thread in between. Stick a small picture on the star.

3. Down on the farm

A4 card: birch green (305) and pine green (339) • Hexagon Coluzzle template • Cutting sheets: AK 009 and AK 010 • Black thread • Double-sided adhesive tape • Butterfly from mini cutting sheet: 3D AM 1004

Make the card according to the instructions. Tie a black thread vertically and cut out the smallest Coluzzle hexagon. Stick a butterfly on each hexagon and stick them to each other with the thread in between.

4. Sun, sea and sand

A4 card: honey yellow (243) and azure (393) • Rectangle Coluzzle template • Cutting sheets: AK 011 and AK 012 • Black thread • Blue glitter pen

Cut the Coluzzle template sideways out of the card. Tie the kite to the thread.

1.

2.

3.

4.

Window cards

You can use Suus and Sam to make funny cards.

General information

Follow the instructions given in Techniques, point 3 and look at Step-by-step photograph 2. Place the template on the card with the barriers horizontal. Place the knife in the desired groove and cut from barrier to barrier. Draw a straight line along the barriers and cut the shape out. If you also wish to have vertical bridges, draw them on the template yourself.

Fold the square card double and cut off 1 cm from the side and bottom edges so that the card measures 15.5 x 15.5 cm. Stick the picture frame on the card using foam tape and make an attractive 3D scene.

1. Watering flowers?

Red square card (517) • A4 card: sunny yellow (247) and royal blue (427) • Circle and square Coluzzle templates • Mini scallop figure scissors • Suus and Sam cutting sheet: DK 801 • White photocopy paper
Place the square template on the blue card with the barriers horizontal. Also draw vertical barriers in the middle of the template. Cut groove 3 from barrier to barrier. Remove the template, draw the straight lines and cut out the squares. Use the Art knife to cut along the outside edge of the template to make a picture frame. Cut grooves 1 and 2 of the template in yellow card and stick the frame on the card using photo glue. Use the figure scissors to make white curtains and stick them behind the windowpanes. Make four circles using groove 7 of the circle template and stick them in the middle of the windowpanes.

2. Going for a dip?

Pastel blue square card (413) • A4 card: royal blue (427) • Circle and square Coluzzle templates • Suus

and Sam cutting sheet: DK 815 • White and blue gel pens

Use the outer edge of the square template to cut out the picture frame. Place the circle template in the top left-hand corner so that groove 4 touches the sides. Cut groove 5. Do this in each corner, so that the circles fit exactly in the picture frame. Remember to only cut along the horizontal barriers.

3. Be careful!

Birch green square card (305) • A4 card: pine green (339) and fawn (241) • Square and rectangle Coluzzle templates • Mini scallop figure scissors • Circle punch • Suus and Sam cutting sheets: DK 817, DK 811, DK 816 and DK 810

Place the rectangle template on the dark green card and cut groove 1. Place the square template in the middle with the barriers vertical, so that two squares can be cut out using groove 6. Remember to only cut from the barrier to the corner. Do not cut the sides, because these are folded open to make shutters. Use the figure scissors to make white curtains and stick them

behind the windowpanes. Cut grooves 2 and 3 of the rectangular template in fawn card and stick this on the picture frame. Fold the shutters open. Use the circle punch for the holes on the shutters.

4. Merry Christmas!

Dark green square card (309) • A4 card: red (517) and silver mirrored card • Square and circle Coluzzle templates • Sticker sheets: stars and silver lines • Silver gel pen • Suus and Sam cutting sheets: DK 805, DK 807 and DK 808

Place the square template on the red card and use the Art knife to cut around the outer edge. Place the circle template in the top left-hand corner so that groove 5 touches the sides. Cut groove 6. Do this in every corner. There will be just enough space left over in the middle for another circle. Cut the mirrored card so that it is slightly smaller than the red picture frame and stick it on the green card. Stick the red picture frame on top of this. Decorate the card with line stickers and stars. Draw decorative lines.

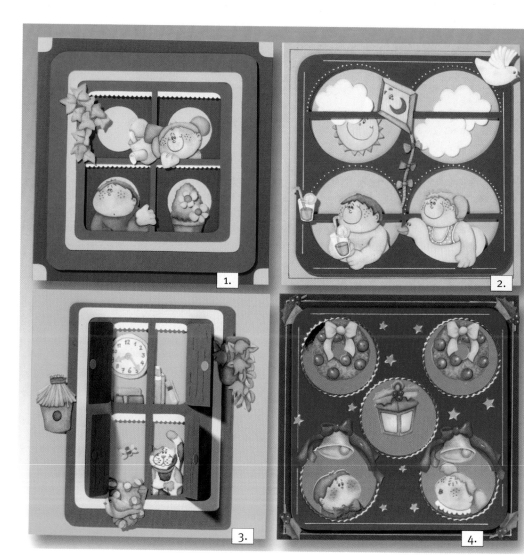

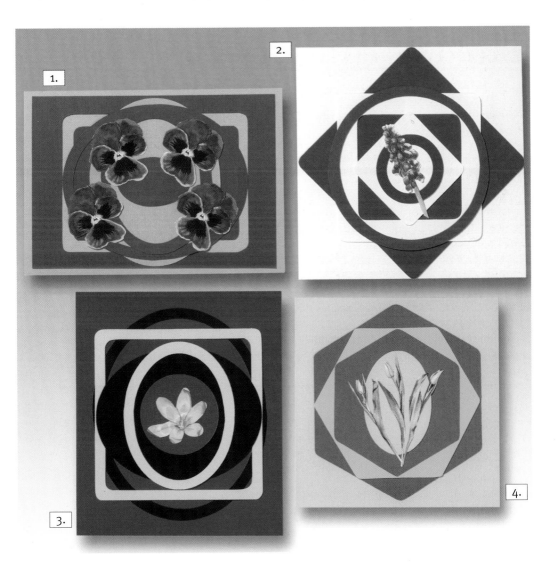

Cards from scraps

You can make the following cards from all your scrap pieces of card.

General information

The size of the cards depends on the size of the scrap frames and shapes.

1. Violet card

A4 card: crimson (549) and mango (575) • Scraps from the oval and rectangle Coluzzle templates • Shake-It cutting sheet: IT 329
The double mango card is placed horizontally and measures 11 x 16 cm.

2. Grape hyacinth card

A4 card: white (211) and royal blue (427) • Scraps from the square and circle Coluzzle templates • Shake-It cutting sheet: IT 348
The white double card measures 14 x 14 cm.

3. Crocus card

A4 card: red (517), sunny yellow (247) and black (219) • Scraps from the square, circle and oval Coluzzle templates • Shake-It cutting sheet: IT 343
The red double card measures 12.5 x 14.5 cm.

4. Tulip card

A4 card: sunny yellow (247) • Green scraps from the hexagon Coluzzle template • Shake-It cutting sheet: IT 327
The double card measures 12.5 x 12.5 cm.

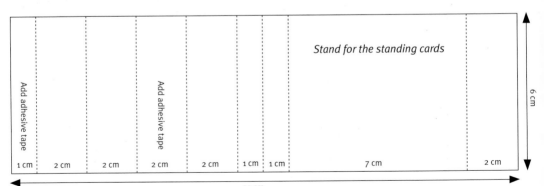

Stand for the standing cards

Add adhesive tape

Add adhesive tape

1 cm | 2 cm | 2 cm | 2 cm | 2 cm | 1 cm | 1 cm | 7 cm | 2 cm

6 cm

20 cm

Hatch cards

The decorated hatches give the cards an extra touch.

General information

Make a card which measures 29.7 x 14.5 cm. Draw a pencil line 4.9 cm from both sides. Draw another line 4.9 cm from the lines you have drawn and score this line. Place the Coluzzle template on the pencil line with the barriers vertical. Cut half of the shape on the left and right-hand sides. Cut away the sections at the top and bottom. Score the cut out part and fold it over (see page 22).

1. Autumn card

A4 card: crimson (549) and mango (575) • Gold line stickers • Insect sticker • Hexagon Coluzzle template • Shake-It cutting sheet: IT 322

Cut grooves 3, 4, 5 and 6 in both the left and right-hand sides of the red card. Grooves 4 and 5 and the middle section are cut out. Cut groove 3 in the mango card and stick it behind the red card.

2. Christmas card

A4 card: dark green (309) and red (517) • Diamond Coluzzle template • Cutting sheet: 3D 370 • Shake-It cutting sheet: IT 370 • Gold gel pen • Relief gloss

Make this card in the same way as the Autumn card, but use the diamond template. The berries are accentuated using the relief gloss. Allow the gloss to dry properly.

3. Butterfly card

A4 card: sunny yellow (247) and pine green (339) • Oval Coluzzle template and oval Companion • Gold line stickers • Stamens • Cutting sheet (3D 374)

Cut grooves 2, 3, 4 and 5 of the oval Companion template in the left-hand side of the yellow card. Grooves 3 and 4 and the middle section are cut out. Cut half of the oval shape in green card using groove 2 and stick it behind the yellow card. Cut grooves 2, 3, 4 and 5 of the Coluzzle template in the right-hand side. Again, cut out grooves 3 and 4 and the middle section. Cut half of the shape again in green card and stick it behind the yellow card. Decorate the card with line stickers and stick the stamens under the butterflies.

4. Violet card

A4 card: dark blue (417) and lilac (247) • Silver line stickers • Shake-It cutting sheet: IT 342 • Circle Coluzzle template and circle Companion

Make this card in the same way as the butterfly card, but use the Coluzzle template on the left-hand side and the Companion on the right-hand side.

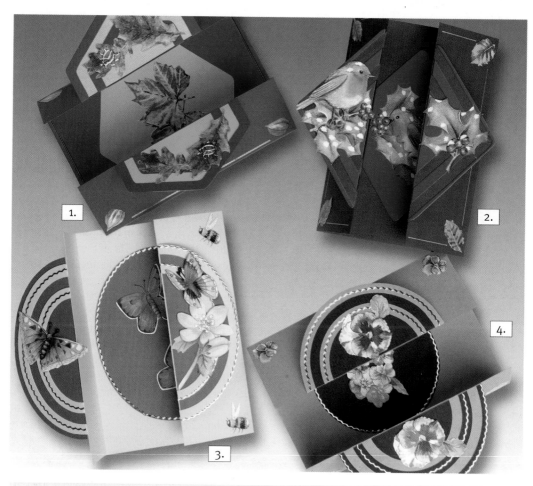

Special thanks to Kars in Ochten, the Netherlands, for supplying the materials.

The materials used can be ordered by shopkeepers from:
Kars & Co B.V. in Ochten, the Netherlands.